MARTIAL ART BASICS

# karate

KEVIN HEALY
5th Dan JKA

Grange
BOOKS

PLEASE NOTE:
The author, packager and publisher cannot accept any responsibility for injury resulting from the practice of any of the principles and techniques set out in this book. If you are in any doubt about your fitness or ability, please refer to a medical professional before trying any of these techniques.

Published in 2008 by Grange Books
an imprint of Grange Books Ltd
35 Riverside, Sir Thomas Longley Road,
Medway City Estate, Rochester,
Kent ME2 4DP
www.grangebooks.co.uk



British Library Cataloguing-in-Publication data available on request.

ISBN 978-1-84804-022-9

1 3 5 7 9 10 8 6 4 2

AN EDDISON•SADD EDITION
Edited, designed and produced by
Eddison Sadd Editions Limited
St Chad's House, 148 King's Cross Road
London WC1X 9DH
www.eddisonsadd.com

The text and illustrations in *Martial Art Basics: Karate* were previously published in card deck form in 2005 by Connections Book Publishing (UK), Barnes & Noble Books (US) and Gary Allen (Aus).

Phototypeset in Zurich using QuarkXPress on Apple Macintosh

Printed in Singapore

MARTIAL ART BASICS

# karate

# CONTENTS

# INTRODUCTION

## Why Karate?

Karate is a dynamic, explosive and highly rewarding martial art that combines physical fitness with mental and spiritual training. Ideal for all ages and abilities, it has something to offer everyone.

If you want sport and competition, Karate can offer this. If you want to know what it feels like to break a stack of tiles, Karate can offer this. But above all, when you begin your Karate journey, you are throwing down a challenge to your mind, body and spirit – a challenge that will build strength of character and help you to overcome your fears. It is a challenge that will ultimately prove to shape your life.

This book is the perfect way to supplement your training, whether you are taking up Karate for the first time or already have some training under your belt. All the basics are presented step by step with clear instructions, and there are hints and tips throughout, to help you make sure you're getting it right. The book is an ideal training aid, and can be used any time and anywhere – so now there's no excuse for not practising your technique!

## In the beginning

'Karate' is, literally, the 'art of the empty hand' (*kara* meaning 'empty', and *te* meaning 'hand'). But why did the need for empty-hand fighting arise?

The islands of Okinawa in the North Pacific became a prefecture of Japan in 1879, after which a law was passed banning the possession of all weapons, in an attempt to reduce the threat of revolt. The Okinawans turned this to their advantage, adapting their own indigenous arts to combine them with those that had filtered through from China. These were the beginnings of the art we know today.

In 1922, Gichin Funakoshi, the founder of modern Karate, was invited to Japan to give a demonstration.

His display was so well received by the public that he decided to remain in Japan and teach his art. A training hall (*dojo*) was built, and the building became known as the *Shotokan* (*Shoto* was Funakoshi's pen name, and *kan* means 'training place').

This, for me, sums up the beauty of Shotokan Karate: nothing is superfluous, from its name, which is direct and to the point, to the type of training, which is hard, demanding and also to the point. It is the most widespread style of Karate practised around the world today. I have been practising it now for more than twenty-five years, and it continues to be both challenging and rewarding, as I hope it will be for you.

## What to expect from a class

Firstly, don't be surprised by the mix of grades. Most clubs are not large enough to run classes solely for beginners, so you could find yourself lining up alongside black belts. This shouldn't be a problem because a good instructor will be able to cater for you as well as for the senior students. And don't worry if you feel nervous to start off with – it will help to keep you on your toes.

Each class will start with a formal bow to the instructor, followed by a general warm-up to prepare you for what will come next. Classes are roughly one to two hours in duration and usually run as follows.

### • Basics

This involves the practice of stances, blocks, punches, strikes and kicks. Depending on grade and ability, these will either be done individually or in combination. Movements are done slowly to begin with, allowing the student to pay attention to detail, and then power and speed are increased so that the final repetitions can be performed with full force.

## • Kata

These are set sequences of moves, best compared to a gymnast's floor display, and part of the class time will be devoted to them. *Kata* practice would be a book in its own right, so we will only touch on it briefly here. There are twenty-seven kata in the Shotokan style, each designed to develop a particular area of training, be it agility, balance, coordination … and the list goes on. In the kata, the student (*karate-ka*) blocks, kicks and punches imaginary opponents, and the order and direction of each move is set.

The initial kata a student will learn are compulsory, and closely linked with the grading system, but as your standard improves you will find that there are also more advanced kata that are optional. There are many to choose from, according to your preference: some are designed to build strength and stamina; others, speed and dexterity.

## • Kumite

After the kata you will move on to sparring, in which students pair off and put into practice the basics learned earlier in class, to hone their fighting skills. There are several types of sparring, the first two of which are covered in this book: *sanbon kumite* (three-step sparring), *ippon kumite* (one-step sparring), *jiyu ippon kumite* (semi-free one-step sparring) and *jiyu kumite* (freestyle sparring). Three-step sparring introduces beginners to pairing-up work. The attacker announces the area he intends to attack, then delivers three consecutive attacks to that target; the defender blocks these, then counter-attacks after the third block. Attacker and defender then swap roles and start again. One-step sparring is the next stage. Here, the attacker announces the target area but only delivers one attack, and the defender blocks and counters immediately. By this stage, the defender will have numerous blocks and counters at hand, making his kumite highly inventive.

Regardless of the type of sparring, certain factors remain constant, and should always be borne in mind: spirit (never give in!), distance (too close, and you will have little or no time to react; too far away, and your counter will be ineffective) and timing.

The class will finish with some stretches to warm down – vital to help prevent stiff muscles from wreaking havoc! – followed by a bow to your partner and, finally, a formal bow to the instructor. Please bear in mind that this format isn't set in stone, as methods will vary from teacher to teacher. However, I always think that a good karate-ka can think on their feet, so it always pays to expect the unexpected.

# Finding a dojo

Today there are numerous clubs in existence, thanks to the explosion in martial arts interest in recent years, but the drawback of this is that these clubs are not subject to regulation. So how can you tell the good from the bad? As a general rule, avoid flashy instructors who make outlandish claims! But aside from this, there are several things you can do.

First, when trying to find a dojo, look around and investigate as many clubs as possible. Always sit and watch a class first; if the instructor won't allow you to do this, ask yourself why. Look at the way the class is run. Is it well organized? Does the class seem well disciplined? Ask questions of both the students and the instructor. How often should you train? What is the grading system? Is the club affiliated to a national governing body? What are the fees? Are you insured? A club secretary will be more than willing to answer these questions.

The most important thing is to find a good teacher – and, when you do, stick with them. *Sensei* means 'teacher', but this is not just restricted to the physical movements of Karate. The Sensei should also lead by example in their manner, their spirit and in the way they conduct themself. Karate is all about training the body in unison with the mind. Find a teacher who offers this; they do exist.

## Stick with it

Once you have joined a dojo, you may find that everything you are taught feels totally alien to you. Don't let this put you off – almost everyone who dons a Karate *gi* (suit) for the first time feels like a fish out of water for a while. To begin with, much of what you are taught will feel far removed from reality, but these early stages are the building blocks, so don't neglect them. Take time to study them properly: only through hard training and constant repetition will you have any chance of mastering the basics. It's also important to stick with one style of Karate; flitting around between clubs can only harm your progress. Don't become a jack of all trades, master of none; focus on your Karate, develop it, refine it. The Japanese have a saying: 'He who hunts two rabbits rarely eats rabbit pie.' Sensible advice indeed.

Remember also that as a white belt you are – in Karate terms – the lowest of the low. Showing respect to your seniors and correct etiquette in the dojo are vital in your development as a karate-ka. Each dojo has its own rules, and these will be explained to you. Don't start off with the attitude that these rules are only for when you're wearing your gi: always conduct yourself in a calm, mature way. Training in the dojo is preparation for the real world.

## Dojo etiquette

First things first: make sure your clothing is clean, presentable and well maintained at all times, whether it's a gi or not. Karate is all about self-discipline, so if you can't manage this, you're in trouble!

If it's your first time, let the instructor know (although they will probably have already guessed!) They will tell you where to stand, and give you a few words of advice. Always address the instructor as 'Sensei' in the dojo, and bow whenever you enter or leave the hall. You must also bow when you face a partner for pairing-up work. Never raise your voice in the dojo and, if you have questions, ask them at the end of the class. Listen closely, and copy what's going on. And don't be put off if you're partnered with a senior-grade student – they will have better control, so you'll actually be less likely to get hurt.

And here are some more pointers … You will be expected to train at least twice a week if you wish to grade. Always show respect to your seniors, and use the word *oss* to show you understand if they offer you advice. Never wear a belt for a grade you have not attained, and never leave the class without permission from the instructor. Also, if you are unable to attend a training session, you should let your instructor know.

## Grading

Probably the most common question new students ask is, 'How long does it take to get a black belt?' The answer is always the same: it's up to you. If you train regularly and reach the required standard for each grade, it generally takes most people roughly three to four years. The route to black belt in the Shotokan system involves ten gradings under a senior examiner. The levels below black belt are called *kyu* grades, and the belt colours work as follows:

| | | | |
|------|--------|-----|---------------------------|
| 10th | *white* | 5th | *purple* |
| 9th | *orange* | 4th | *purple/white stripe* |
| 8th | *red* | 3rd | *brown* |
| 7th | *yellow* | 2nd | *brown/white stripe* |
| 6th | *green* | 1st | *brown/double white stripe* |

You must wait at least three months between kyu gradings, and a minimum of six months between 1st kyu and black belt, to allow for preparation time. Each examination tests your knowledge of basics, kata and kumite, and will be progressively longer and more physically demanding. You will also be tested on elements from previous gradings to make sure you're still working on your basic techniques. Once you pass black belt you become a *Sho Dan*, first black belt, and will no longer grade at your parent club. But that is a long way off; for now, stay focused on your next challenge, and keep your black-belt dreams in check!

## Training regime

Success lies in regular training, and establishing a realistic training regime is the only way that you will advance. Ultimately it comes down to the simple truth that, if you want to train, you will. Of course, if you're married with three kids, it's unlikely that you'll be able to train five times a week, so just set yourself a realistic schedule and stick with it. Even if you're only able to train once a week, just make sure you give 100 per cent every time you put on your gi.

Push yourself in your training sessions – and, when you think you've had enough, push yourself some more. Your body can do more than you think it can. Above all, spirit is the key. Inspiration can come from a few simple words of encouragement from your instructor, so listen and learn.

You also need to accept that development often comes in fits and starts. We all go through stages where our training doesn't go as well as it should. My advice is just to put it behind you. Always maintain a positive attitude – just put it down to a bad day at the office. Karate is hard; it's meant to be. The quicker you set your mind to accepting this fact, the happier you will be. Just give it your all in each class, and you won't go far wrong.

## Maximizing your potential

When training, it's not enough just to know the moves, getting from point A to B without falling over. A karate-ka must understand how to make the body work to its maximum potential, so here are some things to take into consideration:

### • Kime

Prior to every move, be it a kick, punch or block, the body should be in a relaxed state to allow you to react in the quickest possible time. At the point of impact, the whole body should tense as strongly as possible. This focus of power is called *kime*. Techniques without kime, no matter how much they may look like Karate, are imposters.

### • Zanshin

You also need to remain alert prior to movement. This state of mind is called *zanshin* – the state of mental readiness. You may just be standing in *yoi* (ready stance), or pausing between clashes in kumite, but the mind must never switch off.

### • Speed

A technique without speed will have little effect, but work on your technique first; as your Karate improves, so should the speed of delivery. Basic moves often fail as a result of a karate-ka telegraphing their intentions by adding extra movements. Train to give nothing away, and this will greatly enhance the speed of your attack.

### • Kiai

This is the Karate shout, used at certain points in basic training, focal points in the kata, and upon striking an opponent in kumite. It is the link between the mind and the body, and should come from the stomach, not the throat. It should be short, aggressive and embody your total commitment, being used only at the point of greatest focus.

### • Breathing

Breathe out sharply at the moment of focus (don't make it too vocal!), emptying the body of air. This state lasts for only a moment, but is vital. Make sure your stomach is tensed to absorb a blow.

## About this book

Use the book as and when you need to, to supplement your training. Don't feel that you have to work through it in order; you'll know what aspects of your technique you need to work on at any given time, so choose sections as appropriate. Always read the hints and tips provided – they'll help you to turn a good technique into a great one – and pay attention to the foot diagrams, so that your footwork doesn't let you down. Practice is the key.

# WARMING UP

# Warming up

Before you begin, it is important to warm up thoroughly. When doing the following stretches, start slowly and gently increase the stretch. If at any time you feel pain, release the stretch and relax. Before every class, inform your instructor of any injuries you have. It is equally important to warm down at the end of a Karate session. A bit of effort now, and you'll avoid a lot of pain later.

It is a good idea to supplement your Karate with other forms of exercise, to build up your strength. The fitter you are, the quicker you'll recover after exercise and the less tired you will become during training.

▲ SIDE BEND This stretch loosens the muscles down the side of the body. Take the left hand and place it on your hip, then stretch your right arm above your head and lean over. Keep your knees bent and your back straight. Repeat on both sides. Don't reach too far to start with; as you get warmer, reach further.

▲ FRONT BEND Here we stretch the main muscle groups in the backs of the legs, and you will feel the stretch in your shoulders too. Start by placing your feet apart at a comfortable distance. Keep your knees straight and slowly bend forward, placing your hands on the floor. If you aren't supple enough to reach the floor, don't worry – just go as far as you can without too much discomfort. You will feel the stretch down the back of the legs. Hold the position for a few seconds, then slowly release and come up.

◀ **BACK STRETCH** This one does what it says! Stand with your feet apart and your hands over your head (you might find it helpful to hold your right wrist with your left hand, or vice versa). Then lean back slowly to loosen your back. Don't go too far or you may lose your balance. Make sure you keep the neck relaxed so you don't strain it.

▼ **STRAIGHT-LEG STRETCH** Beginners often struggle with this one as it requires some balance. Again we are stretching the muscles in the back of the leg, and at the same time stretching the muscles around the groin. To start, bend the right knee and straighten the left leg. Once in position, stretch the left leg out to increase the stretch. If you then want to increase the stretch even further, take your chest down towards your knee. Do this slowly and don't bounce. You will definitely feel this one stretching down the back of the leg.

▲ **THIGH STRETCH** This stretch is used to loosen the hips and stretch the muscles in the inner thigh. Don't press on the knees and don't bounce them, either. Press the soles of the feet together and then slowly let your knees fall towards the floor. If other people offer to press your knees down, don't let them! This will almost always cause injury.

▲ **FLOOR SPLITS** Sit on the floor and then push your legs apart as if to make the splits. Keep your legs straight and don't bend the knees. When you have found a position that you feel comfortable with, take the chest down to the centre and try to place it on the floor, then repeat on the right leg, then the left. Don't worry if you can't get all the way down – most people can't – but work at it and you will be surprised how much this stretch increases your flexibility. To help with this stretch, you can take hold of your ankles and pull yourself gently forward.

**KNEE LIFT** ◄ Lift the knee, then take hold of the shin and pull your leg in toward your body as far as you can. This will help your knee lift when you kick, and at the same time stretch the leg muscles. Another good one for balance, this one. Repeat on both legs.

**OUTSIDE-LEG STRETCH** ▼ A bit of a dancer's stretch this one, but great for stretching the limbs and loosening the hips. It also helps develop balance. This is not an easy stretch, so if you are struggling with it you can miss it out and move on to another one.

**STRETCHING TIPS**
- Don't stretch too hard, too soon.
- Try to get the body warm before attempting the stretches – a short run or a bit of skipping will do the trick.
- Always stretch at the end of a class. This will help prevent the legs and hips stiffening up in the following days.
- Make sure you stretch both sides of the body equally – don't just concentrate on one side.

▼ SQUAT THRUSTS For this strength-training exercise, make the push-up position – legs outstretched, back straight. Then pull your legs in so that the knees touch your elbows. Don't lift up, and keep your hips down. Now thrust the legs out to their initial point, and repeat several times. This exercise is excellent for developing your fitness.

## Making a fist

For your punching to be strong and effective, you must first learn how to make a correct Karate fist (*see below*). After that, it's down to you to condition it into a powerful weapon through your training.

**1▶** Stretch the hand out flat, with the palm facing downwards.

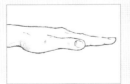

**3▶** Now roll the fingers so that they are tightly 'shut' into the palm of the hand.

**2▶** Open the thumb and bend the ends of the fingers over, keeping them tightly together.

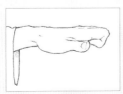

**4▶** Wrap the thumb under the gripped fingers to seal the fist. Keep the wrist straight and the punching knuckles prominent.

# STANCES

# Front stance
## Zenkutsu dachi

Front stance is the first stance taught to a Karate student and the most commonly used stance in Karate training. When making front stance, it is important that the stance isn't too long or too wide. Too long will inhibit movement; too wide, and you will find yourself off balance. At first you will find learning stances hard work, as the positions will seem quite unnatural. They are also very demanding on the leg muscles, but don't give up and make high, weak stances – this will hinder your progress later on. Strong stances make for strong Karate.

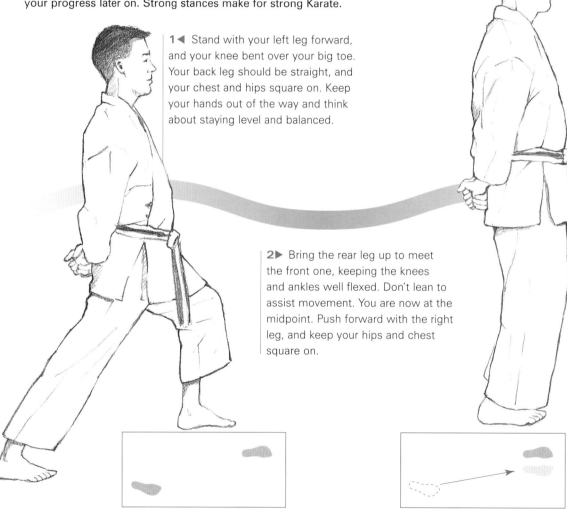

**1◄** Stand with your left leg forward, and your knee bent over your big toe. Your back leg should be straight, and your chest and hips square on. Keep your hands out of the way and think about staying level and balanced.

**2►** Bring the rear leg up to meet the front one, keeping the knees and ankles well flexed. Don't lean to assist movement. You are now at the midpoint. Push forward with the right leg, and keep your hips and chest square on.

**3◄** As your right foot lands, strongly lock the supporting leg, while at the same time making sure your front knee is well bent and aligned over your toes. Check your hips and chest are square on. To step again, repeat the sequence on the opposite side.

### Front View
The legs should be hip-width apart. Check that the upper body isn't leaning to the left or right. You will often hear Japanese Sensei shouting 'Push stomach', meaning 'Keep your body straight, don't lean.' To check if your stance is deep enough, look down at your front leg: if you can see your big toe, you are too high, so bend a little more until your toe is hidden by your knee.

### REMEMBER
- Always keep your back straight – never lean.
- When moving, keep at the same level. Don't move up and down.
- As you start to step, push off hard through the rear leg, like a sprinter out of the blocks. At the midpoint, as your feet meet, use the supporting leg to drive you on.

# Back stance
## Kokutsu dachi

Back stance is one of the hardest movements to master in Karate, and because of this it is often neglected. The difficulty arises from the fact that the movement is alien to most people. Back stance demands that the karate-ka works with his heels in line, making balance awkward. As well as having 70 per cent of the weight on the rear leg and 30 per cent on the front leg, the knees must be pushed out at right angles to one another and the hips must be kept level. Back stance is found in nearly all kata, so it is vital to come to terms with it at an early stage in your Karate training or your kata will suffer.

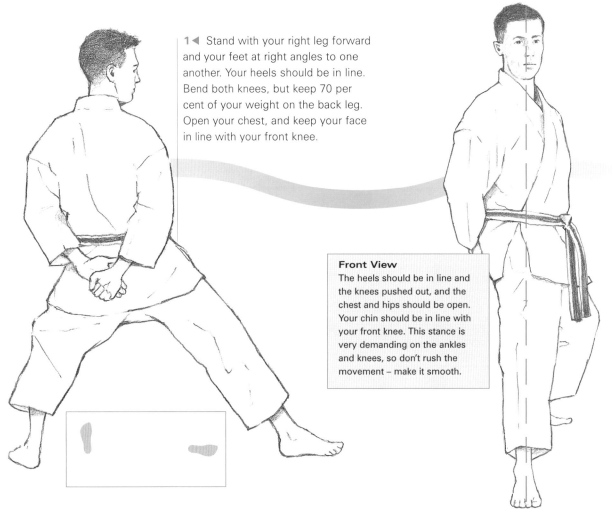

**1◄** Stand with your right leg forward and your feet at right angles to one another. Your heels should be in line. Bend both knees, but keep 70 per cent of your weight on the back leg. Open your chest, and keep your face in line with your front knee.

**Front View**
The heels should be in line and the knees pushed out, and the chest and hips should be open. Your chin should be in line with your front knee. This stance is very demanding on the ankles and knees, so don't rush the movement – make it smooth.

## REMEMBER

- Don't make the stance too long or the rear knee will dip inwards. Remember to push out the knees.
- Don't stamp when stepping.
- There is a tendency to lean backwards in this stance, so make sure you keep both hips level.
- Start slowly and work on smooth movement on a level plane.

3▼ Slide your left foot into place, and as you do so twist your hips and turn the supporting foot out, pivoting on your heel. The heels should now be in line and the knees pushed up and out at right angles to each other, with the weight distribution 70/30 from rear leg to front leg.

2◀ Bring the rear leg up to meet the front one, keeping the knees and ankles well flexed. Don't lift up as you move. You are now at the midpoint. Step forward with the left leg, keeping the sole of the foot close to the floor. Don't raise the heel of the supporting leg as you start to move – this will cause loss of power.

# Horse stance
## Kiba dachi

Horse, or straddle-leg, stance is similar to back stance in that the heels are in line, only here both feet are turned in and the knees are pushed out. This aids balance. It is particularly demanding on the legs and knee joints, but is a very powerful stance, and you should feel rooted to the spot when it is executed correctly. Always keep your back straight and don't fall into the trap of leaning back. At first you will find it very tiring on the leg muscles, but (as with all Karate training) don't give in and come up out of the stance – stick with it and reap the rewards.

**NOTE**
This stance has three kata (formal exercises) built around it, and so is of great importance in the Karate grading syllabus. Do not neglect it.

**REMEMBER**
- Stretch well before using this stance, as it makes great demands on the muscles and joints.
- You should always feel that the weight is evenly proportioned between both legs.
- Avoid moving up and down when delivering the technique – keep level.

**1◄** Stand with your left leg forward, heels in line, and your feet slightly inverted. Grip the floor with your toes. Centre your weight and bend the knees, pushing them outwards, creating tension in the legs.

**3◄** Now step out with the left leg into horse stance. As you land, turn your feet in and push your knees out. Remain at the same level throughout the movement.

**2▼** Bring the rear leg up to meet the front one but, unlike in front and back stance, don't freeze at the midpoint – carry on and cross the legs over. Keep the knees well bent and your back straight.

**Side View**
Note the feet are in line, with the toes turned in, gripping the floor. The knees are bent and pushed out, creating tension in the legs. Keep your back straight, and always face the direction of travel. When moving, don't lift upwards – keep your knees bent, and glide through.

# PUNCHES

# Straight punch
## Choku zuki

Straight punch is the classic Karate punch, delivered in a straight line, the fist travelling inverted from the hip but rotating on impact. Correct timing is essential, so start slowly but with feeling. Don't just think of the punching arm – develop the returning arm too, so that even standing still you are developing your whole body. When practising Karate, no movement should ever be done casually. Even when working slowly on a punch, do it with the correct mental attitude and attention to detail. Working in slow motion can be used to great advantage as a type of resistance training.

**1◄** Stand with your feet apart (Hachiji Dachi position). Hold your left arm out in front of you in line with your solar plexus, and your right fist, inverted, just above the hip bone. You should be relaxed but alert.

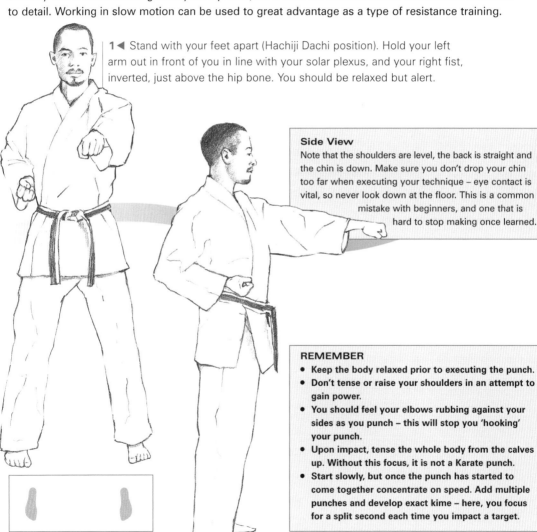

**Side View**
Note that the shoulders are level, the back is straight and the chin is down. Make sure you don't drop your chin too far when executing your technique – eye contact is vital, so never look down at the floor. This is a common mistake with beginners, and one that is hard to stop making once learned.

**REMEMBER**
- Keep the body relaxed prior to executing the punch.
- Don't tense or raise your shoulders in an attempt to gain power.
- You should feel your elbows rubbing against your sides as you punch – this will stop you 'hooking' your punch.
- Upon impact, tense the whole body from the calves up. Without this focus, it is not a Karate punch.
- Start slowly, but once the punch has started to come together concentrate on speed. Add multiple punches and develop exact kime – here, you focus for a split second each time you impact a target.

**3▼** Drive the punching arm out while at the same time withdrawing the reaction arm. Don't let your shoulders rise up. It is vital you don't twist either fist yet – leave that to the last moment, when you complete the punch with maximum focus (kime).

**4▼** Now fully extend the punching arm, rotating the fist at the very last moment. Simultaneously, the reaction arm should be returning to your side, twisting strongly back into an inverted position. Remember – maximum tension at the moment of striking.

**2▲** Keeping your shoulders down, slowly drive your right fist out towards the target. At the same time, begin to withdraw the extended arm. At this midpoint the elbows should be against your sides.

# Stepping punch
## Oi zuki

Stepping punch is generally one of the first techniques students learn. It combines the delivery of the basic Karate twisting punch with the use of the front stance. It is one of the most direct and powerful techniques in Karate, as it involves a strong stepping action combined with the karate-ka using his full body weight. No momentum or balance is lost in spinning, making it a commonly used attack.

> **REMEMBER**
> - Keep your back straight and eyes up, looking straight at the target. Never overreach.
> - If you step too slowly, your opponent will have time to evade the punch, so always keep it quick.

**1◄** Put your left foot forward in the downward-sweeping-block stance (*see page 48*). This stance is commonly used as the starting point for many of the techniques. Shift your weight onto your front foot, in preparation for moving your back leg and, as you start to step, push your right heel into the ground to help propel you forwards.

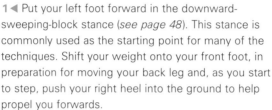

**2►** Pull the rear leg up alongside the front leg, keeping level as you move. The hips should now be square on. Don't straighten your legs – keep both knees and ankles well flexed, so they can act like springs to propel you forwards as you punch. Hold your right elbow tight against your side, to help keep the punch straight. Hold your left arm forwards horizontally.

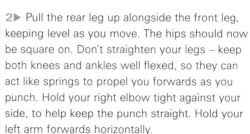

**3▼** Keeping the hips and shoulders square, step forwards with your right leg into front stance. At the last moment drive the punching arm (right) out to the target. Simultaneously pull the reaction arm (left) back strongly. Just before you are about to strike the target, rotate the punching fist. Remember to tense the fist and wrist and to strike with the two prominent knuckles (*see Strike Area, right*). Only tense your body at the point of impact, so you don't telegraph your intentions.

### Strike Area

Note that the thumb is held well back out of the way to avoid injury. Use it to help bind your fist together. The knuckles of the index and middle fingers (known as *seiken*) are used to strike the target.

### Side View
Twist the fist through 180 degrees at the very last second to give maximum kime (focus) to the point of impact. On completion of the punch, the whole body should be square on, driving the full body into the attack. Note how the back leg remains straight when the punch is executed.

# Reverse punch
## Gyaku zuki

Reverse punch is one of Karate's most popular techniques. It is regularly used in kumite (sparring), as it is easily deployed as a counter-attack. It is essential when delivering this punch that the hips and chest are only employed at the very last moment prior to impact with the target, to maximize power.

**1◀** Put your left foot forward in the downward-sweeping-block stance (*see page 48*). Keep your chest and hips at an angle of 45 degrees from the direction you are facing – they don't come into play until the moment of punching.

**2▲** Without moving the chest and hips, start to make right-hand reverse punch by moving your punching arm forwards and pulling your reaction arm back. Keep your elbows close to your sides to avoid hooking the punch.

**Side View**
Don't just concentrate on rotating the right hip and side of your chest as you punch. If, at the same time, you pull your left hip and side of chest back along with the recovery of the reaction arm, this will greatly speed up the punch as well as add further power. This pushing and pulling of the body is vital in developing true Karate. Note that the front knee is now fully committed.

**3▲** Now fully extend the punching arm, and push your hips and chest into the technique to maximize power. At the same time, pull the reaction arm back to your side. Tense the back leg strongly to absorb the impact of the blow when it lands. Make sure you are punching to the centre, in front of your solar plexus. Note the width of the stance: too wide, and you won't be able to use your hips correctly when you punch; too narrow, and the rotation of the hips and chest will take you off balance.

**REMEMBER**
- **The punch must land at the same time as the hip twist – easier said than done, as the hand has much further to travel. Correct timing is everything with this technique.**
- **'Keep face.' Anyone who has trained regularly with the Japanese will have heard this expression. Basically, don't take your eyes off your opponent. Even when your body twists, don't let your head turn with it.**

# Leading-hand punch
## Kizami zuki

Leading-hand punch is delivered with the front hand (the hand on the same side as the forward leg in front stance). Normally executed to the face, this punch can best be described as a stopping technique, in that as your opponent starts to attack you move in and take the initiative, punching to the face before the attacker has time to deliver his own attack.

**1◄** Place your left leg forward in front stance, and your right arm forward in reverse downward-sweeping-block position (*see page 48*). Make sure your hips are square and the left elbow is pulled tightly to the side of the body.

**2►** Keeping your left elbow pressed tightly against your side, start to punch. Keep the punching fist inverted and don't start to move the chest and hips yet. As with reverse punch, the rotation happens at the last moment.

**3▼** The split second before impact, rotate your hips and chest to 45 degrees and twist the punching fist. This rotation increases your reach to the target. Also, to add power, push your left knee towards the opponent. Don't forget to draw the reaction arm back to your side, inverting the fist, and tense the body strongly on impact. The two punching knuckles should be aligned directly in front of your chin.

**REMEMBER**
- **Don't allow your front elbow to stick out as you punch; this will take the punch off line, as well as damage the elbow joint.**
- **On impact make sure the muscles around the shoulders and sides are tensed strongly to absorb the blow.**

**Side View**
Note that the punching fist is in line with the chin. When attacking to the head in basic training, always aim for your own head height.

# STRIKES

# Back fist strike
## Uraken uchi

Back fist strike has two variations. In the first it travels in a circular action to the temple; upon striking the target it returns via the same route. In the second it again takes a circular motion but this time in a downward direction, striking the bridge of the nose. The striking area is the back of the hand.

**REMEMBER**
- Don't lose control of the striking elbow, as this controls the attack.
- Don't just rely on the snap of the strike for its effectiveness; make sure you get your hips and chest into the strike for maximum power.

**1▼** Stand in front stance, left leg forward, with your guard held in the freestyle (kamae) position. Your elbows should rest against your sides, and your body should be held at 45 degrees to offer less of a target.

**2▶** Step with the rear leg to the midpoint. At the same time, pull your right fist to the left side of your face in preparation for the attack. Push the reaction arm out, but keep your shoulders down and body square.

**Strike Area**

Don't hit with the back of the hand. Use only the conditioned area – the knuckles – when you strike.

**Front View**
The striking fist is in line with the chin. The body twist increases reach and maximizes power.

**3▲** Extend the right arm in a snapping action and attack to the side of the jaw, keeping your elbow firmly in place. As you strike, twist your body to 45 degrees, and pull the reaction arm back to your side.

**4▶** Snap the attacking arm back as soon as you have executed the strike. From here, lower the hands to freestyle position. Throughout the attack keep the snapping elbow still, to maintain control.

# Palm-heel strike
## Teisho uchi

As your Karate training develops, you will discover that the fists and feet are not the only weapons. Palm-heel strike utilizes the heel area of the hand: the wrist is bent back, with the fingers and thumb tightly clenched. This method of attack is usually aimed at the jaw. Upon striking the target, the fingers can then reach out and attack the eyes. This is a close-range attack and a very effective one.

**2▼** Step with the rear leg to the midpoint. Take your right hand back to your hip, bending your wrist back in preparation to strike, and push your left arm out parallel to your chest. The forearm should slope slightly, as though water could run down it. Keep level, and keep your body square on.

**1◄** Stand in front stance with your left leg forward. Hold your guard in the freestyle position, keeping your elbows tucked in. Your body should be at 45 degrees.

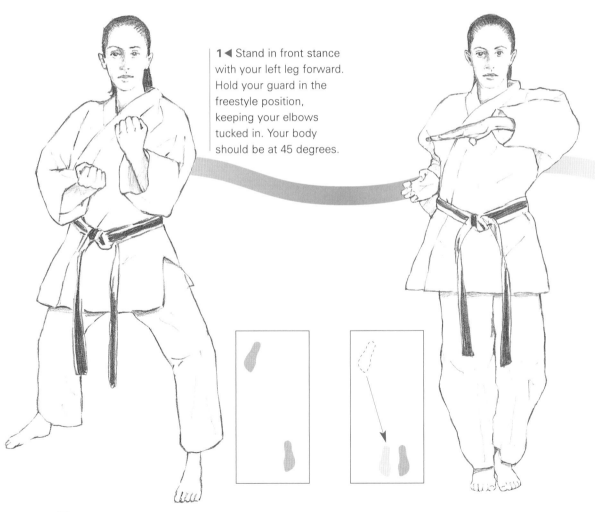

**3◄** Now step forward with the right leg into front stance, and drive the palm heel forwards and upwards towards the opponent's jaw. Be sure to drive your hips and chest into the technique, to give greater force to the strike.

## Strike Area

Pull the wrist back as far as possible, gripping the thumb and fingers tightly back, out of the way. Strike with the heel of the hand.

**Side View**
For maximum effect, drive the strike out as far as you can, locking your elbow joint in the process.

**REMEMBER**
- Start slowly. Make sure you are hitting with the right part of the hand.
- Keep your fingers well out of the way; open, they are easily broken.

# Knife-hand strike
## Shuto uchi

Knife-hand strike uses the outside ridge of the hand as the striking area. This area, from the base of the little finger down to the wrist, is surprisingly strong. Often when karate-ka demonstrate breaking techniques (tamashiwara), this is one of the strikes used. The power for this technique comes from the circular route of the attack. The knife hand is normally aimed at the throat or neck. Great care must be exercised when carrying out this technique, as the open hand can easily catch the opponent in the eyes.

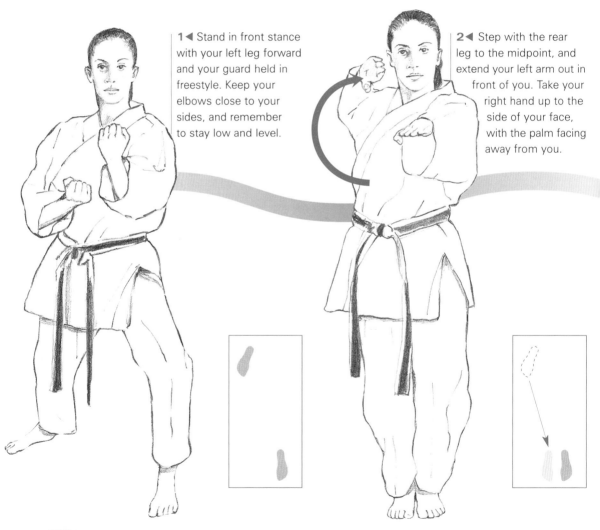

**1◄** Stand in front stance with your left leg forward and your guard held in freestyle. Keep your elbows close to your sides, and remember to stay low and level.

**2◄** Step with the rear leg to the midpoint, and extend your left arm out in front of you. Take your right hand up to the side of your face, with the palm facing away from you.

**3▼** Step forward with the right leg and attack with the right arm to the neck. Your left arm should simultaneously return to your left hip. Make sure your hips and chest are turning in time with the attack.

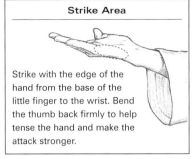

**Strike Area**

Strike with the edge of the hand from the base of the little finger to the wrist. Bend the thumb back firmly to help tense the hand and make the attack stronger.

**REMEMBER**
- Keep the thumb well bent, as this helps strengthen the wrist area when striking.
- Even though the knife-hand attack will feel strong due to its circular route, make sure you are still getting your hips into the movement for maximum force.

**Side View**
As the hand is about to strike the target, invert the wrist sharply using a strong twisting action. Make sure to strike with the ridge of the hand and not the side of the fingers.

# Roundhouse elbow strike
## Mawashi empi

Roundhouse elbow strike, along with the other elbow attacks, is designed for close-in fighting. These strikes are short, fast and devastating if landed without control. Because they are used at close range, it means the opponent has little or no time to see them or get out of the way. Always strive to get maximum force into the technique through fluid use of the hips and chest.

**1◄** Stand in front stance, left leg forward, with your guard held in freestyle. Remember to keep your elbows tucked into your sides.

**2►** Step with the rear leg to the midpoint. Push your left arm out in front of you – this will help to push away your opponent – and bring your right fist back to your hip.

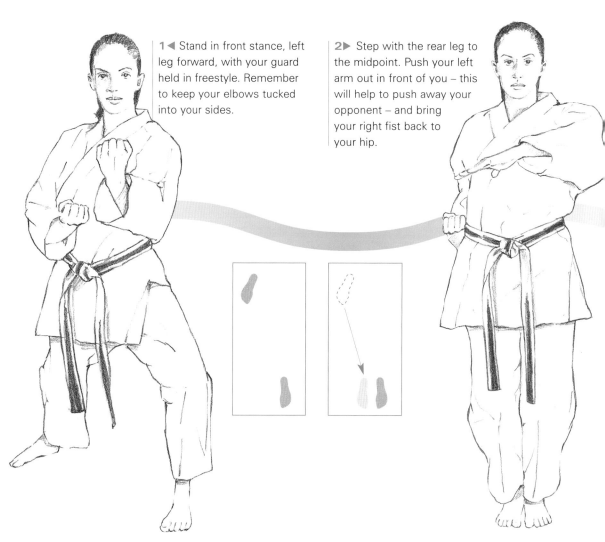

**3▼** Rotate the hips and chest, and at the same time drive the right elbow in a circular action towards the target. Don't let the fist drop, and don't raise the elbow. As the strike lands, place the right fist squarely on the chest. The right arm should travel on one plane.

### Strike Area

Always strike with the point of the elbow, not the forearm. Remember: this is a very strong attack, so good control is essential.

### REMEMBER
- Distance is vital with this attack – make sure you get in close to your opponent.
- The point of the elbow is very hard, so be sure to exercise good control in partner work.

### Side View
The striking arm should travel on one plane when executing this attack.

# Rising elbow strike
## Age empi

Rising elbow strike is designed to attack under the jaw, knocking the head back as it lands. As with all elbow strikes, it should only be contemplated for close-in fighting. Remember: getting in really close to your opponent does have its advantages and is a vital part of realistic training for combat, but don't forget, if you are in range, so is he. The nearer you are to an opponent, the less time you have to react to attacks. Always keep this in mind. The truth is that at some point you will get hit, so be prepared.

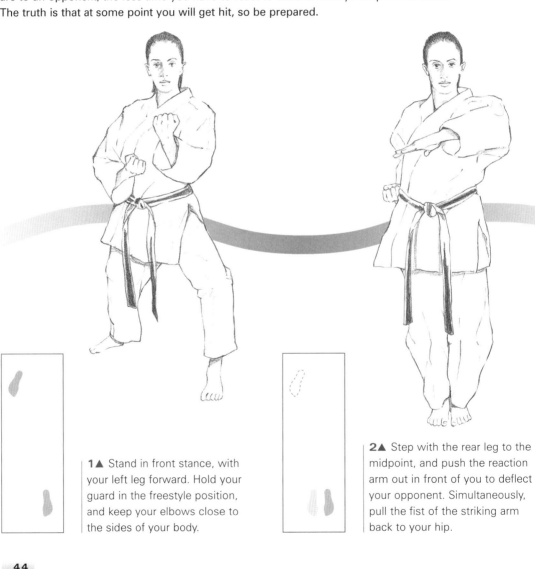

**1▲** Stand in front stance, with your left leg forward. Hold your guard in the freestyle position, and keep your elbows close to the sides of your body.

**2▲** Step with the rear leg to the midpoint, and push the reaction arm out in front of you to deflect your opponent. Simultaneously, pull the fist of the striking arm back to your hip.

**3▼** Step with the right leg into front stance, and at the same time drive the rising elbow up to the target – in this case, underneath the attacker's jaw, pushing the head back. As before, twist the hips and chest into the attack, rotating the body to 45 degrees. When you start the rising elbow attack, try to keep your fist as close as possible to the side of your face, so that it brushes your cheek. This will keep the attack nice and tight.

### STRIKE AREA

Again, strike with the point of the elbow. Try to press your forearm into the bicep to strengthen the attacking arm.

**Side View**
As you complete the strike, drive the elbow as high as you can – your reach should improve with practice.

### REMEMBER
- Keep the striking arm pressed tightly against the side of your face on impact.
- Don't allow your head to turn away as you hit.
- Try to grab hold of your opponent, to stop him escaping or leaning back to avoid the strike.

# BLOCKS

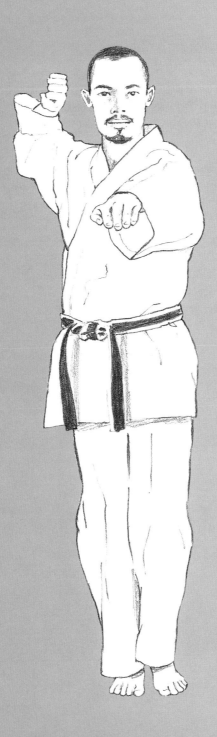

# Downward-sweeping block
## Gedan barai

As you will have already seen, a large part of basic training starts from the left-leg-forward, downward-sweeping-block position. This block is primarily used to defend against mid-section kicks. It is certainly one of the more powerful blocks, as it makes full use of the hips and chest.

**1◄** Stand in front stance, with your left leg forward. Hold your left arm downwards in front of you, in line with your front leg, and hold your right fist (inverted) on your right hip. Your chest and hips should be at 45 degrees.

**2►** Step with the right leg to the midpoint. At the same time take your right fist up to the left side of your face, keeping the elbow pressed down. The left arm should point down to the ground, the hand open, and both arms should be squeezed together. Make sure you haven't lifted up – keep your knees bent.

**3▼** Now step with the right leg into front stance, and at the same time drive the right fist down to block. The left arm should be pulled back to the hip. This movement will help turn the body to 45 degrees. As you land, be sure to lock your back leg. The front knee should be well bent.

**REMEMBER**
- Don't swing the arm down – drive it as though you are striking.
- Make sure you don't block too high. The blocking hand should be roughly the width of a fist above the front knee.

**Front View**
Note that the knees and feet are together and the body is square on. Remember to press your elbows together and keep your shoulders down. Don't let your right elbow rise up – keep the point of the elbow in line with your solar plexus. This position should feel very compact, ready to explode into the block.

# Rising block
## Age uke

Rising block is designed to deflect blows to the head. Upon completion, the blocking arm should be above the head at an angle of 45 degrees. At the same time, the body should twist to 45 degrees to assist deflection of the attack.

**1◄** From ready stance (yoi), step forward into left-leg front stance, and make left-arm downward-sweeping block. Your body should be at 45 degrees.

**2▲** Step with the rear leg, and at the same time point your left arm in front of your face. At this midpoint your body should be square on to the target. Remember not to lift up when you step – keep your knees bent and your shoulders relaxed.

**3▼** Step with the right leg and keep the right fist pinned to the hip until the very last moment. Then, as the foot lands, drive the right fist up from the hip, travelling in front of the face, pulling your left fist back to your side at the same time. The blocking arm should twist over in the same way that a punch does at the point of impact. This twist helps deflect the attack. Both hands should twist together at the last moment.

**REMEMBER**
- Even though you use your arms to block, make sure your feet get you out of danger. Always step quickly.
- Never 'just block'; always train to counter-attack.
- When using the basic blocks, never lean away to avoid the attack. Escaping the attack in this way stops you from testing the effectiveness of the block.

**Side View**
Make sure your hips and chest are now at 45 degrees, allowing you to counter-attack. It's a common mistake with junior grades to look up as the block is executed. Don't. Look directly ahead, and maintain eye contact with your opponent.

# Outside block
## Ude uke

Of the two mid-section blocks, the outside block is the strongest. It is also the block most beginners struggle with. Start slowly and break it down into separate parts, but still attempt to make each movement as fluid as possible. This block really is bone on bone, and it will hurt to start off with, but don't be put off.

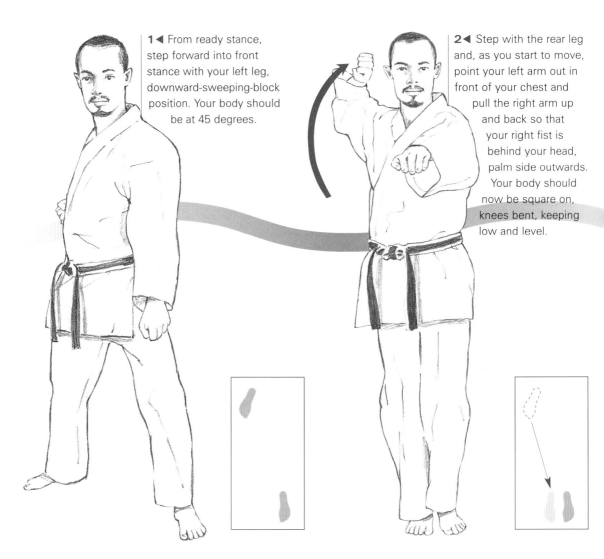

**1◄** From ready stance, step forward into front stance with your left leg, downward-sweeping-block position. Your body should be at 45 degrees.

**2◄** Step with the rear leg and, as you start to move, point your left arm out in front of your chest and pull the right arm up and back so that your right fist is behind your head, palm side outwards. Your body should now be square on, knees bent, keeping low and level.

**3▼** Now step with the right leg. As with rising block, keep the blocking arm back until the last moment. As the right foot lands, drive the right forearm down and across your mid-section, covering the area in front of your chest. Twist the blocking arm at the end of the technique. This block can be used to deflect both kicks and punches.

**REMEMBER**
- Don't reach for the attack – let it come to you.
- Make sure you block with the area just below the wrist.
- Don't block too close to your body, as the blocking area is small, and if you miss the attack you may get hit. Remember: fast feet to evade the attack, and a strong block to deflect it.

**Side View**
As with all blocks, the body travels through 45 degrees, helping to drive the block forward.

# Inside block
## Uchi uke

Inside block is the other mid-section block, and can also be used to deflect both kicks and punches. It is easier to learn than outside block but not as strong, and for this reason it's not used as much in partner work.

**2▼** Step forward with the rear leg, and at the same time extend the left arm in front of your chest, taking your right arm (with the blocking fist) across your body under the left. The fist should sit just above the hip. Your body should be square on and your knees bent, ready to move.

**1▶** Step forward into front stance with your left leg, and make downward-sweeping block with your left arm. Your chest and hips should be at 45 degrees.

**3▼** Now step with the right leg – try to keep the body square on until the last moment. As the right foot lands, block across your chest from the inside out, twisting the hips and chest to 45 degrees to increase power and reduce the target area you are offering your opponent. The blocking fist should finish in line with your front knee.

**REMEMBER**
- Don't block too close to your body, or you may get hit.
- Don't let the block ride up – check that the blocking fist is level with your shoulders.
- When you make the block, control the elbow – don't let it 'wobble', as this will weaken the movement.

**Side View**
The head is up, and eye contact is good. Make sure you don't allow the blocking elbow to get too close to the body, as this will increase your chances of being hit.

# Knife-hand block
## Shuto uke

Knife-hand block is the first open-hand technique a student will come across. The fact that it is used in conjunction with back stance – all other techniques coming from front stance – makes it doubly difficult. The outer ridge of the hand is used to make the block, and this causes two potential problems: first, it is such a small part of the hand that it is easy to miss the target; and second, beginners often injure themselves, blocking with the fingers instead.

**Side View 1**

**1 ◄** Stand in back stance with your left leg forward – check your heels are in line and your back is straight. Your right hand should be inverted, placed covering your solar plexus, and your left arm should be out in front of you with the elbow bent and hand open, palm facing downwards.

**REMEMBER**
- Throughout the block, keep the fingers rigid and the thumbs well bent.
- At the end of the movement, check that your front foot, knee, blocking elbow and chin are in line.
- Make sure you leave the twist in the hands until the very last moment. Don't let your hands just swing to the target.

**3▼** Keeping the hands still, step with the right foot into back stance. Don't let all your weight fall forward and then rock back into the stance as an afterthought – keep the weight on the supporting leg. At the last moment, pivot on the left heel at right angles; coincide this twist with the blocking action of the hands. As you pull the left hand back, drive your right hand down and across from your face, stopping the block in line with the knee. Feel the hands cutting through the air as they twist.

**Side Views**
The feet are at right angles to each other, and the weight is predominantly on the rear leg. The reaction arm should remain open and twist into place on the solar plexus, and the hand should be level with the elbow of the blocking arm. Don't straighten the blocking arm too much, as this will reduce the power of the block – the arm should form a triangle.

**Side View 2**

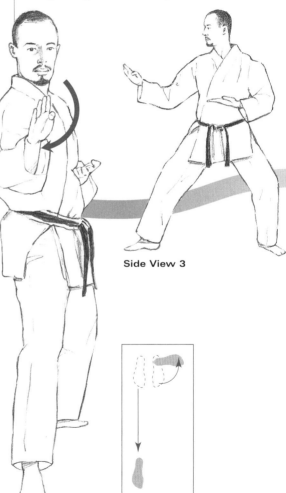

**Side View 3**

**2◄** Step with your right leg to the midpoint and, as you start to step, point your left hand out in front of your chest. At the same time, take your right hand to the left side of your face, with the palm of the hand facing your cheek. You are now square on, knees bent.

# KICKS

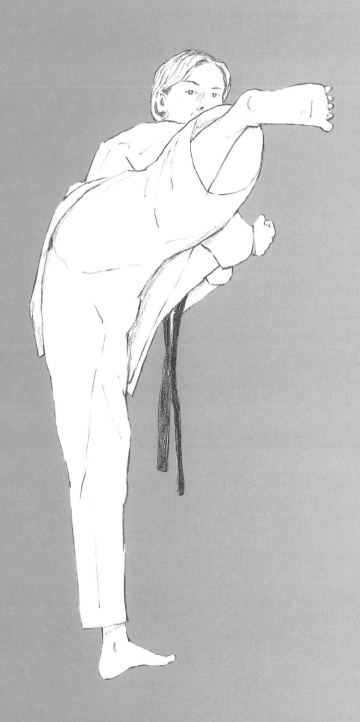

# Front kick
## Mae geri

Front kick is the first kick a beginner is taught. It is the most direct kick, and technically the easiest to grasp. However, in kumite it is the least used of the kicks. This is probably due to the confidence required to execute it correctly. Front kick can be directed to the head, body or groin area (*gedan*).

**REMEMBER**
- When starting the kick, don't telegraph the attack by adding extra movements, such as moving the arms or head prior to the kick.
- Make sure you push both hips into the kick.
- Never lean backwards to gain height – rely on a good knee lift to give your kick greater range.

**1▲** From ready stance, step forward into left-leg front stance. Hold your arms in the freestyle position. At this point, keep the upper body relaxed, especially the shoulders. Any tension here will slow the kick.

**2▲** Without changing guard, height or body position, lift the right knee. As you start to do so, pull the toes back as far as possible on the kicking foot. Lift the knee as high as you can. At this midpoint, make sure the supporting leg is well bent, acting like a spring, aiding balance. Keep both hips square on to the target.

**3▼** Kick out with the right leg, and at the same time push both hips forward into the attack. Strike the target with the ball of the foot. Make sure you don't lock the supporting leg. Remember that your knee is acting like a spring here, so keep it bent to absorb the impact of striking the target.

**4▼** Upon striking the target, snap the kicking leg back to its midpoint position. Feel the calf pressed against the back of the thigh. By doing this you will be sure to have snapped the kick back correctly. A common mistake with kicking is not recovering the leg sharply once the kick has been delivered. This leaves you vulnerable to a counter-attack. Recover the kick quickly, and then you have the option of stepping forward or returning the foot to the starting point.

### Strike Area

Pull the toes back as far as you can and aim to land with the ball of the foot. Remember to point the foot into the attack, so that you don't hit with the sole of the foot.

### Front View
The kick should be straight, in line with your chin. Note the bend in the supporting knee, and that the body is square on – don't let it twist as you deliver the kick.

# Side thrust kick
## Yoko geri

Side thrust kick makes full use of the thrusting action of the leg. The kick is almost always directed to the mid-section, and the point of contact is the side edge of the foot (*sukuto*). This kick is difficult to master as it involves being able to hold the leg out while using a strong twisting action from the supporting leg. You will find this one of the most tiring of kicks. Make sure you have stretched fully before executing it.

**REMEMBER**
- Most people tend to swing the leg to the target or let it ride up. Avoid this by using a very high knee lift.
- This kick is greatly weakened the more you lean away from the target. Try to keep upright. Height isn't important – power and accuracy are.
- This kick demands great muscle control. If you are struggling, use a wall or chair for balance and practise holding the leg out.

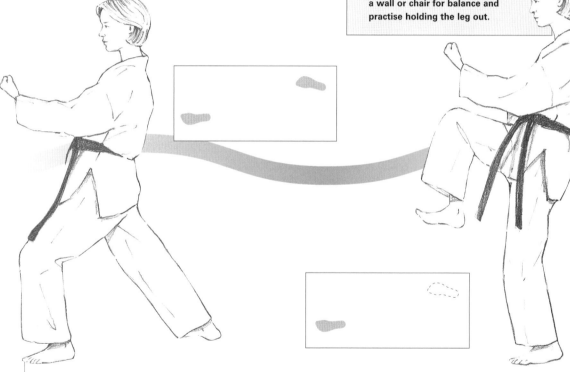

**1▲** Stand in front stance, left leg forward, guard in freestyle position. Before you start to kick, remember to keep level and let your legs and hips do all the work. Don't hold your arms stiffly – they should feel relaxed, with the elbows resting against the body.

**2▲** Lift the right knee as high as you can, while keeping the supporting leg bent. Aim to lift the knee between the gap in your arms so that you don't have to move them prior to kicking, thus telegraphing your intention. As in front kick, pull the toes back as far as you can. Relax your shoulders.

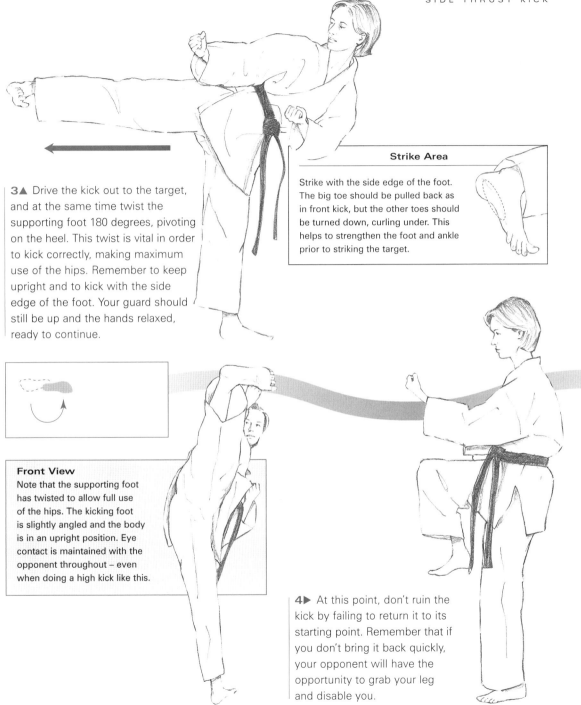

**3▲** Drive the kick out to the target, and at the same time twist the supporting foot 180 degrees, pivoting on the heel. This twist is vital in order to kick correctly, making maximum use of the hips. Remember to keep upright and to kick with the side edge of the foot. Your guard should still be up and the hands relaxed, ready to continue.

### Strike Area

Strike with the side edge of the foot. The big toe should be pulled back as in front kick, but the other toes should be turned down, curling under. This helps to strengthen the foot and ankle prior to striking the target.

### Front View

Note that the supporting foot has twisted to allow full use of the hips. The kicking foot is slightly angled and the body is in an upright position. Eye contact is maintained with the opponent throughout – even when doing a high kick like this.

**4▶** At this point, don't ruin the kick by failing to return it to its starting point. Remember that if you don't bring it back quickly, your opponent will have the opportunity to grab your leg and disable you.

**63**

# Roundhouse kick
## Mawashi geri

Roundhouse kick is one of the more spectacular Karate techniques. It travels in an arc towards the target, unlike the previous kicks, which come straight at you. It can be used to attack either the head or body (*jodan* or *chudan*). Hip flexibility is vital for this kick to be executed correctly. When kicking to the face, train to kick with both the ball of the foot and the instep; the first being the classical interpretation, the latter the competition way. Both have value.

**Side View 1**

**Side View 2**

**1▲** Stand with your left leg forward in front stance, guard in freestyle. Prior to kicking, visualize the target in your mind's eye and focus. You must keep the body as relaxed as possible until the point of impact.

**2▲** Lift the right leg to the side, but don't lean – keep upright. Pull the kicking toes back and keep the supporting leg bent. It is common to lift up at this point, so check this and stay level. Lifting causes loss of balance and makes for a slower attack.

**REMEMBER**
- Be sure to twist the supporting leg as the kick strikes. This will allow you to use your hips as well as gain maximum range.
- There are many bones in the foot and this kick often collides with elbows, so to avoid injury, train for accuracy.
- The instep needs to be conditioned for kicking, which is best done with a kick bag. Start hitting it lightly and make good contact with the flat surface of the foot. When you are happy with this, start to increase speed and power.

Side View 3

**Side Views**

Of all the kicks, roundhouse kick is one of the hardest to break down into stages. You need to make it flow from beginning to end. It is vital that you twist the hips at the right time, otherwise the kick will be greatly weakened. Don't worry about height to start off with – try to develop a smooth action you can control. Note that your kicking foot should travel round in the same plane as your leg.

**3▲** Kick out with the right leg in a snapping action. At the same time, rotate the hips by twisting the rear foot 180 degrees, pivoting on the heel. Don't kick short of the target; when kicking to the head, for example, you should see your foot travel past your face. This way you know you are making a penetrating attack.

**4▲** Snap the kicking leg back quickly. You now have the option of moving forward or stepping back. A common mistake with roundhouse kick is to raise the heel from the floor to gain height; never do this, as you will only execute a weak attack of no value.

# Spinning back kick
## Ushiro geri

Spinning back kick is one of the most challenging kicks because it involves balancing on one leg as you spin, in addition to briefly turning your back on your opponent. Because its delivery must be quick, timing is of the essence and you need a strong supporting leg. When successfully landed, this kick is one of the most powerful, as it uses the momentum of the spin and the driving hips. It is essential not to telegraph your intention to your opponent prior to and during the attack.

**1▲** Step forward from ready stance into front stance, with your left leg forward and your guard held in freestyle. Just before you begin the kick, narrow your stance slightly to allow for a smoother spinning action. You are aiming to complete this whole technique in one fluid motion, without pausing.

**2▲** Draw the kicking (rear) leg closely into the supporting leg, tucking your foot behind the knee. Keep the supporting leg flexed and the hips level – if you lock the supporting leg, or raise your hips, this increases the likelihood of losing your balance, while at the same time indicating to your opponent your intention to kick.

**3▼** Spin your body around 180 degrees in a clockwise direction (the opposite way when kicking with the left leg), pivoting on your heel, keeping the kicking leg tightly wrapped around the supporting leg. Keep your hips level. It is vital that the spin derives from a strong turning action in the hips, and not from turning the shoulders. At the same time, turn your head to look over your shoulder at your opponent.

**4▼** Keeping the supporting leg bent, drive your right leg out at the target, fully extending it. Don't let yourself lean either to the left or the right, as this will cause loss of balance at the critical moment of impact. Keep spinning as you kick out. When the kick is complete, you should finish back facing the direction you started at, having turned a full 360 degrees. Remember to recover the kick quickly, so that you don't leave yourself vulnerable to a counter-attack.

**Front View**

The body remains aligned as the kick is executed, and the attacker maintains focus on her opponent throughout.

**REMEMBER**

- The kick must be delivered in the shortest possible time, as you are putting yourself at a disadvantage by momentarily turning away from your opponent.
- From the moment your foot leaves the floor, make this attack in one fluid action. Any hesitation or added movement will indicate your intentions and give your opponent an opening.
- Take care not to overspin, taking your body round too far and kicking off line.

**Strike Area**

Strike with the heel – point your toes to the floor, flexing your foot to make it rigid. On impact, tense the ankle to absorb the blow.

# COMBINATION WORK

# Sequence 1

This punch–block–punch–block combination is a simple way for a student to practise punching and blocking in a small area. The combination involves stepping, punching and blocking. Each move should involve a hip twist and good stance work. Take care not to rush, and to complete each technique correctly before moving on.

> **REMEMBER**
> - Never lean to assist movement.
> - When making reverse punch, keep your back straight and let the hips and chest create the power.

**2▼** Step punch to the face (jodan). As you land, make sure your body is square on to the target. Check that your back leg is locked.

**1▲** Stand in front stance, with your left leg forward in downward-sweeping block. As you start to step, remember to push off hard with the back leg.

**3◄** Pushing off with the right foot, step back into left-leg front stance. As you land, make left-arm rising block. Remember to twist the chest and hips to 45 degrees. When stepping backwards, don't lean the upper body to help speed up your step – use the leg muscles to propel you.

**4▼** Now counter with reverse punch. As you punch, lock your back leg, rotate your hips and chest and pull the reaction hand back sharply. The torso should now be square on.

**5►** Finish the combination with left-arm downward block. Don't move the hips too soon here. Take the blocking arm up in preparation, and only at the last moment, when you are about to complete the block, turn the hips to 45 degrees. As with all hip movements, the later you leave them, the sharper your Karate will become.

# Sequence 2

This combination is designed to help develop the ability to change direction and stance. The techniques are not in themselves the issue. Later, when you are more familiar with the sequence, change the techniques around to avoid it becoming stale and unchallenging. A true karate-ka should be able to move and change direction with ease. Train to be fluid.

**2▼** Step with the back leg and make stepping punch to the mid-section (chudan). Remember to stay level – don't lift up in an effort to gain speed or power. Lock the legs on impact.

**1▲** Stand in left-leg front stance. Again, remember to push off with the back leg when you step.

**3▶** Open the right palm, withdraw the left fist to the side of the face and, pushing off with the right heel, step back and make left-arm outside block. As you land, twist the body to 45 degrees. The block should finish at the same time as the step. Remember: even though you have stepped back, you must thrust your weight forward on completion of the block. Keep the front knee well bent.

**4◄** Prepare to strike with the elbow (*Empi*). Keeping your hips level, slide your left foot back to the right one, at the same time opening the blocking fist and stretching it away from you, palm up. Keep your face to your opponent and your shoulders down.

**REMEMBER**
- Step 4 is a midpoint. When attacking, only hold this position for a moment, then make the attack. As your skill increases, this midpoint will last a mere fraction of a second.
- Keep level. No extra power is gained by bouncing up and down.
- Keep as much tension as possible in the legs, to create a power stance as you strike. Remember to turn your feet in and push your knees out. And don't lean back.
- When you deliver the strike, don't lift up – a common mistake. Stay low and push your hips and chest into it.

**6▼** From this position, strike with the back of the fist (*Uraken*). Once the attack is complete, snap it back as in position 5.

**5▲** Now attack with the point of the elbow, sliding the left foot out into horse stance. Remain level. Only as the knees push out and you complete the stance should you strike with the elbow. Note that the open hand has now become a fist and rotated on impact.

# Sequence 3

This combination appears difficult. It is. Use it to develop a high level of balance and hip flexibility. It doesn't really matter what kicks you use; whatever you choose, try to mix them up and create problems for yourself.

**REMEMBER**

- Don't hold the fists too tightly as you kick. This will create tension and slow you down.
- When kicking off the front foot, don't lean back to help get the foot off the floor. Also, leave the back foot where it is – don't slide it in and make a shorter stance. That's cheating.
- The height of the kicks doesn't really matter at this stage. Get the technique right and worry about high kicks later.
- This is a difficult combination. Make it smooth and flowing, and try to avoid jerky movements.

**1▲** Stand left leg forward in front stance, guard held in freestyle.

**2▶** Keeping the back straight, lift the front foot and make left-leg side thrust kick. Keep your face to the target and your arms and upper body relaxed.

**4▼** From this standing position, now quickly lift the right knee to the side and make roundhouse kick. Remember to pick your knee up as high as possible and not to lean away to get greater height. Snap your kick back, but keep your knee up.

**3▲** Recover the kick, keeping a high knee lift, then drive the left foot down so it sits beside the right. Keep your knees bent. To complicate things, add a right-arm downward-sweeping block as you land. The block should finish as the foot hits the floor. Focus is vital, so be sure that the body tenses at this moment.

**5▶** Now drive the right knee down and make right-leg front stance. At the same time as you land, push the left side of your body forwards and make left-arm reverse punch.

# Sequence 4

This combination uses kicks, blocks and strikes. Don't rush the initial attack so as to speed up the sequence. Finish each technique off as you would deal with an attacker, then move on. Remember: it's not the number of moves executed but the quality of each technique that exemplifies advanced Karate.

**REMEMBER**
- Throughout the combination, keep face with your opponent.
- Keep the supporting leg bent when you kick. This will stop you lifting up when you kick and perhaps losing balance.
- When striking with rising elbow attack, keep the arm pressed tightly to the side of the head.
- Strike with the point of the elbow.

**1▲** Stand in front stance, left leg forward, guard held in freestyle.

**2▲** Lift the right knee and attack with front kick. Don't alter your guard or telegraph your intention by adding extra movements.

**3◄** Recover the kick with a strong snapping action, hold your balance and then step forward into right-leg front stance. As you land, deliver a rising elbow strike.

**5▲** Focus your stance for a moment and check your balance. Now, without moving the rear leg, lift the front knee and kick left-leg side thrust kick. Once the kick is finished, recover with a strong knee position and then step forward into front stance.

**4►** Pushing off through the right foot, step back with the right leg, making left-leg back stance knife-hand block. As you land, make sure you have shifted your weight on to the rear leg and your heels are in line.

## Sequence 5

This final combination is set to develop hip flexibility and balance as well as kicking accuracy. When kicking, always aim at a target. Don't fall into the trap of losing focus when practising basics – always imagine an opponent and strike a defined target; never lash out blindly.

**2◄** Use your right hand to attack with knife-hand strike, to the side of the face. Push your chest and hips into the attack. To increase power, pull the reaction arm back strongly to the left hip.

**1▲** Stand with your left leg forward in front stance, and your guard held in freestyle position.

**3◄** Leave the striking arm out and deliver a right-leg front kick, to the mid-section. Don't drop the right arm as you kick: hold it focused in place – it's not easy.

**4◄** Keeping the hips level and the supporting knee well bent, recover the front kick with a snapping action. At the same time rotate the body clockwise 180 degrees and wrap the right foot behind the left knee. You are now ready to attack with spinning back kick. Make sure you maintain eye contact with your opponent even though you have your back to them.

**REMEMBER**
- When attacking with knife-hand strike, remember to keep the thumb well bent, as this strengthens the wrist.
- When practising the change from front kick to back kick, allow yourself to stop at the midpoint to correct your balance. Later, as skill improves, try to make the sequence one fluid action.

**5►** Drive the right heel out to the target, keeping the upper body relaxed. Spinning back kick is often executed to the head (jodan), but the body (chudan) offers a greater target area, which is something to bear in mind. Lock the kicking knee strongly on impact.

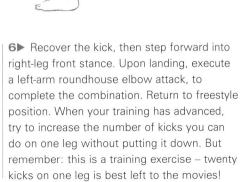

**6►** Recover the kick, then step forward into right-leg front stance. Upon landing, execute a left-arm roundhouse elbow attack, to complete the combination. Return to freestyle position. When your training has advanced, try to increase the number of kicks you can do on one leg without putting it down. But remember: this is a training exercise – twenty kicks on one leg is best left to the movies!

# THREE-STEP AND ONE-STEP SPARRING

# Head attack

In three-step sparring, both attacker and defender have a role to play. When you attack, ensure your opponent has to block. When you block, make sure the block works. When counter-punching, use maximum force and intent but make sure you control the technique; if you don't, it will finish your opponent. It is for good reason that Ippon is often referred to as 'the killing blow'.

DEFENDER    ATTACKER

**2▼** The attacker calls 'jodan', to announce the target area, then steps and punches to the face with the right arm. At the same time, you retreat and make rising block. Make sure you block wrist to wrist.

**1▲** Stand upright in ready stance. The attacker stands in left-leg front stance. Make sure you are standing close enough for there to be a real chance that the attacker will step in and land his punch. Learning the importance of distance is vital.

**3▶** The attacker again makes stepping punch to the face, this time with the left arm. Step back and make right-arm rising block.

**4▶** The attacker makes his last stepping punch to the face. Step back and block with your left arm. At this point, you should both check that you are close enough to make an effective counter.

**REMEMBER**
- On each occasion of blocking, the defender must rotate his body to 45 degrees to reduce the target area offered to the attacker. This is vital in preparation for the counter-attack.

**5▼** Now counter-attack with right-hand reverse punch. Aim for the solar plexus. Be sure that the hips and chest are timed with the strike. As you hit the target, make a strong kiai.

# Body attack

Again, correct distance is vital. The attacker should never feel that he can't reach, and the defender should always be close enough to counter the moment an opening occurs. Although this sequence is taught as the most basic form of partner work, done correctly it can be extremely challenging. The attacker should vary the speed and rhythm of his attack and, as defender, try standing closer to reduce your reaction time and create more pressure for yourself. Training must push you to the limit if it's to have any value.

DEFENDER     ATTACKER

**1▲** Stand in ready position. The attacker stands in front stance, left leg forward. The attacker calls 'chudan', announcing the target area.

**2▲** The attacker steps forward and makes chudan stepping punch to the mid-section. Step back with your left leg and block with a right-arm outside block.

**3▼** The attacker advances again, punching to the mid-section. Step back with the right leg this time, and make outside block with the left arm.

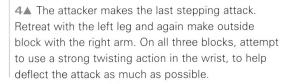

**REMEMBER**
- Make sure you don't hang around in position 5, which is a midpoint. Prepare to attack, then attack. Karate must be realistic, and if you pause your opponent won't.

**4▲** The attacker makes the last stepping attack. Retreat with the left leg and again make outside block with the right arm. On all three blocks, attempt to use a strong twisting action in the wrist, to help deflect the attack as much as possible.

**6▲** Now strike to the attacker's solar plexus, pushing out with the right leg into horse stance. As you strike the target, tense the legs strongly, to absorb the impact. Remember to use kiai.

**5▶** Slide your right foot back. At the same time prepare to attack with roundhouse elbow strike, using the right elbow. Remember to keep level as you slide out, and to keep your face to your opponent.

# Head attack

The distance needed to block is not always the same as that required to counter. In this sequence the defender has to make a stance change to allow the use of the kick. Getting this right takes years of practice – start slowly and work on fluid movement.

DEFENDER            ATTACKER

**2▼** The attacker shouts 'jodan' and then makes stepping punch to the head. Step back with the right leg and make left-arm rising block.

**1▲** Stand in ready stance. The attacker stands in left-leg front stance. The onus is on the attacker to check that he is close enough to make an effective attack (in other words, one that has to be blocked).

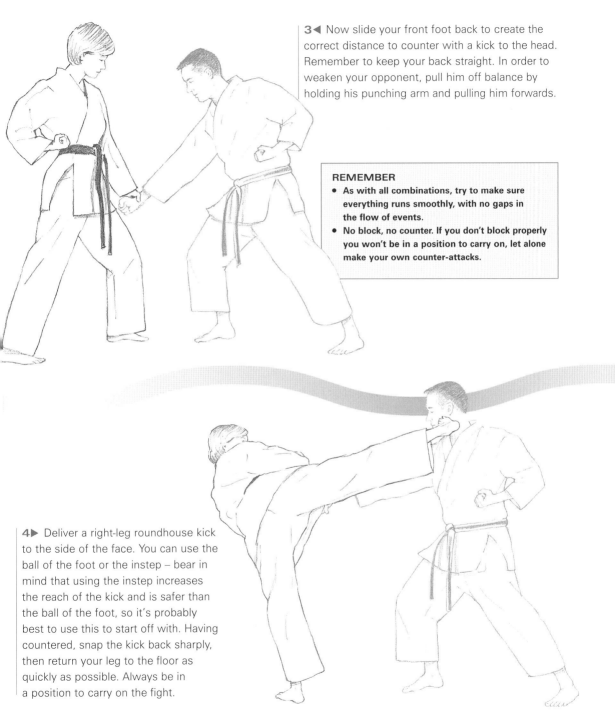

**3◄** Now slide your front foot back to create the correct distance to counter with a kick to the head. Remember to keep your back straight. In order to weaken your opponent, pull him off balance by holding his punching arm and pulling him forwards.

**REMEMBER**
- **As with all combinations, try to make sure everything runs smoothly, with no gaps in the flow of events.**
- **No block, no counter. If you don't block properly you won't be in a position to carry on, let alone make your own counter-attacks.**

**4►** Deliver a right-leg roundhouse kick to the side of the face. You can use the ball of the foot or the instep – bear in mind that using the instep increases the reach of the kick and is safer than the ball of the foot, so it's probably best to use this to start off with. Having countered, snap the kick back sharply, then return your leg to the floor as quickly as possible. Always be in a position to carry on the fight.

# Body attack

In this sequence the attacker counters with spear hand (Nukite). Great care must be taken with open-hand techniques as they can easily damage the eyes – one of the reasons for keeping nails short! Spear-hand attack is often neglected but it is, nonetheless, a very real attack when it strikes the intended target area.

DEFENDER

ATTACKER

**2▲** The attacker shouts 'chudan', then makes stepping punch to the mid-section. Step back with the right leg and make left-arm downward-sweeping block.

**1▲** Stand in ready stance. The attacker stands in front stance, left leg forward. Attacker: don't look down or away. Develop the confidence to look directly at your opponent and let him know you mean business.

## Strike Area

It is said that spear hand was developed in order for a karate-ka to be able to defend himself against an opponent wearing armour. The spear hand would be aimed at the joints in the armour where narrow targets presented themselves. Today it is most commonly seen in kata, but is still a valid weapon when aimed at the eyes, throat or solar plexus. To 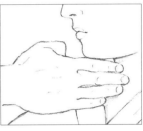 execute it correctly demands years of conditioning, so don't try this technique until you feel confident in your Karate. A strong wrist is vitally important to avoid the hand buckling on impact.

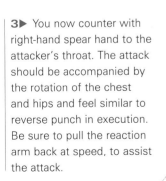

**3▶** You now counter with right-hand spear hand to the attacker's throat. The attack should be accompanied by the rotation of the chest and hips and feel similar to reverse punch in execution. Be sure to pull the reaction arm back at speed, to assist the attack.

# PRACTICE
# SPARRING

# Front kick (1)

The following pages show sparring techniques for use against specific attacks. Here the defender has the chance to counter with two hand techniques: one to the face, one to the body. Train to make the delay between counters as small as possible. Many students, for whatever reason (though usually pain), kick off target. Don't allow this, or you won't know if your blocks are working.

> **REMEMBER**
> - The more you unbalance your opponent with your block, the less chance they will be in a position to fight back, and the longer you have to counter-attack.
> - Block as strongly as possible; the pain this inflicts often softens up an opponent and weakens their resolve.
> - It's not easy to find the solar plexus under a Karate gi, so find your own using a prod of your finger and apply this knowledge to your opponent. It is used as a target area because, unlike the stomach muscles, it can't be built up. You will know when you hit it!

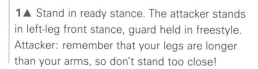

**2▶** The attacker shouts 'Mae Geri', and then attacks with a right-leg front kick to the stomach. As she attacks, step back with the right leg and make left-arm downward-sweeping block. As you block, try to knock the attacker off balance so that she is disoriented for a moment.

**1▲** Stand in ready stance. The attacker stands in left-leg front stance, guard held in freestyle. Attacker: remember that your legs are longer than your arms, so don't stand too close!

**3◀** As the attacker lands with her right leg forward, draw your left fist to the side of your face and then counter-attack with back fist strike, to the attacker's jaw.

**4▼** The moment the strike lands, counter with reverse punch to the solar plexus. Ensure you make full use of the chest and hips on the reverse punch, and maintain maximum focus (kime) as the punch lands.

# Front kick (2)

In this sequence the defender combines a step with the right leg with a left-arm block not only to parry the attack but also to help draw the attacker on to the counter. This requires great skill. Remember that the attacker's head will be meeting the counter-kick, so watch your control. The golden rule is that if you are close enough to hit, you are also close enough to *be* hit.

DEFENDER          ATTACKER

**1◄** Stand in ready stance. The attacker stands in front stance, left leg forward, guard held in freestyle.

**REMEMBER**
- Kicks are generally heavy and hard to block. Don't rely on brute force to defeat them. Always attempt to get your body out of the way just in case.
- If you can take the attacker off balance when you block, all the better, as this will create a window of opportunity for you to counter.
- As with all combination counters, work slowly to start with: make it work, then apply the speed. Be sure to return the kicking foot to the floor at speed, but don't rush and thus make the kick less effective.

**3◄** Now attack to the head with left-leg side thrust kick. Remember to lock the leg but to aim a fraction short of the target, for safety. If you are not that confident kicking to the head, then attack to the body.

**4▼** As the leg recovers, step forward into front stance and attack with roundhouse elbow strike, to the solar plexus. Drive the hips and chest into the attack for maximum effect.

**2◄** The attacker shouts 'Mae Geri', then delivers a front snap kick to the stomach. At the same time, step out with your right leg and make downward-sweeping block with your left arm. This step takes you away from the attack, so if the block were to fail the attacker would kick thin air as opposed to your ribs. This is a good opportunity to knock the attacker off balance.

# Side thrust kick (1)

This block and counter works just as well whether the attacker kicks to the face or body. Attempt to use the block to spin your opponent round, thus exposing the kidneys and spine. You need maximum attention to control when attacking these areas. As a rule, the legs are heavier and stronger than the arms, so don't rely too heavily on the block. Make sure you step away quickly, to avoid the kick.

DEFENDER    ATTACKER

**1◄** Stand in ready stance. The attacker stands in front stance, left leg forward, guard held in freestyle.

**REMEMBER**
- Attacker: try to develop a side thrust kick that isn't easily deflected. Use a partner to try to knock you off balance as you kick – it works wonders.
- As with all combinations, work to a point where there is no gap between the fist hitting the target and the foot leaving the floor to strike to the body (chudan).
- When you kick, remember that you have the choice of using the instep or ball of the foot. Practise with both.
- When blocking the attack, attempt to spin the attacker so that he has his back to you. This gives you a large target area and stops him from blocking your counter.

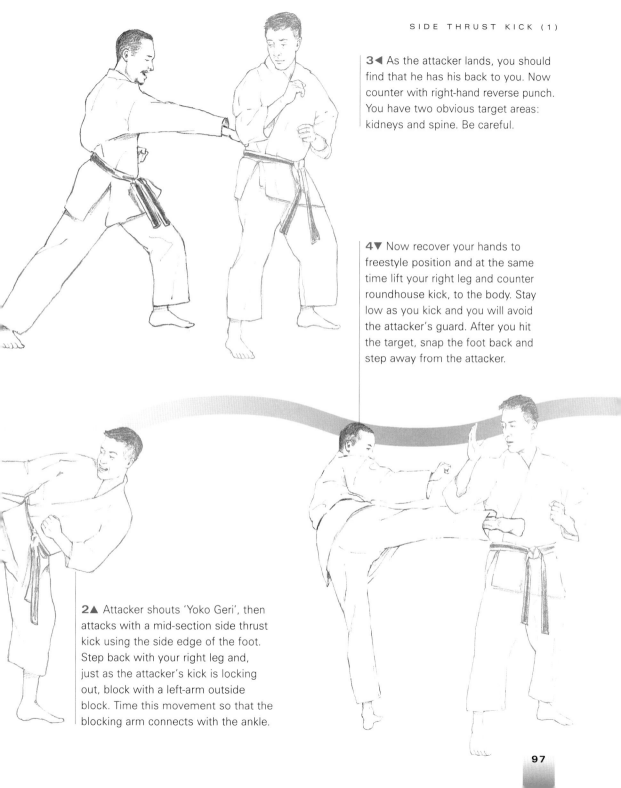

**3◄** As the attacker lands, you should find that he has his back to you. Now counter with right-hand reverse punch. You have two obvious target areas: kidneys and spine. Be careful.

**4▼** Now recover your hands to freestyle position and at the same time lift your right leg and counter roundhouse kick, to the body. Stay low as you kick and you will avoid the attacker's guard. After you hit the target, snap the foot back and step away from the attacker.

**2▲** Attacker shouts 'Yoko Geri', then attacks with a mid-section side thrust kick using the side edge of the foot. Step back with your right leg and, just as the attacker's kick is locking out, block with a left-arm outside block. Time this movement so that the blocking arm connects with the ankle.

# Side thrust kick (2)

In this sequence the defender puts together a foot, then a hand, counter. The most important thing is to make sure the initial block works. Remember: no block, no counter.

**REMEMBER**
- When kicking off the front foot, don't lean back to assist the knee lift, as this will weaken the kick.
- If you find yourself too far away to kick after blocking, make up the distance by sliding up the back foot. Remember to keep level, though.
- It's important to get the timing of the block right: catch the ankle, not the back of the leg.

DEFENDER    ATTACKER

**2▼** The attacker calls 'Yoko Geri', then attacks with a right-leg side thrust kick to the mid-section. You react to this by stepping back with the right leg and blocking the kick with left-arm outside block.

**1▲** Stand in ready stance, with the attacker in left-leg front stance, guard held in freestyle.

**3◄** As the attacker lands, counter-attack with side thrust kick to the mid-section. Here the kick will be with the left leg, coming off the front foot. Remember to strike with the edge of the foot and to lock the leg. Think about driving the kick through your opponent.

**4▼** Now recover the kicking leg and step forward into front stance, at the same time striking to the side of the head with knife-hand strike. Don't forget to twist the striking hand on impact, and to be aware of good control when attacking this vulnerable point.

# Roundhouse kick (1)

In this combination the defender again has to deal with a kick, but then counters using the palm-heel strike. A new problem raises its head here in that a roundhouse kick – because of its circular route to the target – follows the defender as he attempts to step inside it. Consequently, timing the step and block correctly is vital.

> **REMEMBER**
> - Keep the wrist strong – it's easy to injure the joint.
> - Apply basic principles when attacking, such as hip and chest rotation and maximum use of kime.
> - Don't rush these attacks – make sure you are hitting the correct target and can control the technique.

DEFENDER      ATTACKER

**1 ▲** Stand in ready stance. The attacker steps forward into left-leg front stance, guard held in freestyle.

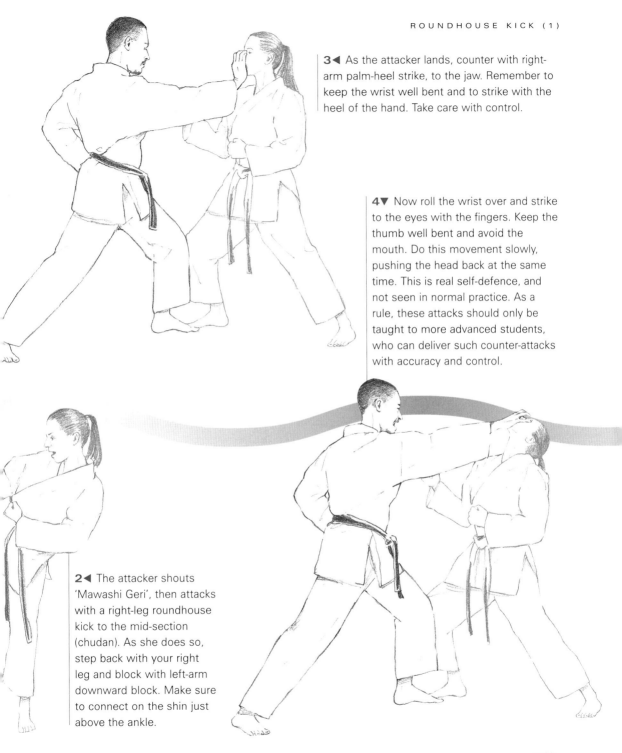

**3◄** As the attacker lands, counter with right-arm palm-heel strike, to the jaw. Remember to keep the wrist well bent and to strike with the heel of the hand. Take care with control.

**4▼** Now roll the wrist over and strike to the eyes with the fingers. Keep the thumb well bent and avoid the mouth. Do this movement slowly, pushing the head back at the same time. This is real self-defence, and not seen in normal practice. As a rule, these attacks should only be taught to more advanced students, who can deliver such counter-attacks with accuracy and control.

**2◄** The attacker shouts 'Mawashi Geri', then attacks with a right-leg roundhouse kick to the mid-section (chudan). As she does so, step back with your right leg and block with left-arm downward block. Make sure to connect on the shin just above the ankle.

# Roundhouse kick (2)

In this sequence the defender has to avoid a roundhouse kick. The golden rule here is always try to get inside the kick; this will prevent the attacker penetrating your guard, while at the same time opening up the attacker to a counter.

> **REMEMBER**
> - Hitting someone in the stomach can wind them. This will tend to bring the head forward rather sharply; if you are then countering to the face, be aware of this and be sure to control your counter.
> - When making inside block against roundhouse kick, don't step back in a straight line – step off to 45 degrees. This will get you out of the way and create a bigger target area for when you counter.

DEFENDER        ATTACKER

**1▲** Stand in ready stance with the attacker left leg forward in front stance, guard held in freestyle.

**2▶** The attacker shouts 'Mawashi Geri jodan', then attacks with a roundhouse kick to the head. At the same time, step back with your right leg and make left-arm inside block.

**3▶** As the attacker lands, slide the front foot back and counter-attack with roundhouse kick to the mid-section. Make contact with the ball of the foot, and try to hit the solar plexus if you can.

**4▶** Once you have snapped the kick back, step into your opponent and strike to the face with back fist strike. This is a very fast, snapping attack and it's easy to leave the hips and chest out while you execute it. Don't.

# Back kick (1)

Due to the fact that back kick is a fast, strong attack, it does pose problems for a defender. If you aren't switched on, you will find that the kick has hit you before you have time to react. Stay alert and, the moment the attacker spins, step out of the way.

**REMEMBER**
- Once you have the sequence worked out, attempt to block the back kick, and then counter-attack with your own kick without delay. The attacker should be knocked off balance and then hit as he lands. Give him no time to react.
- When you counter with front kick, the blow may bring the attacker's head forward in an involuntary movement. This is good, but remember that as the head comes forward your elbow strike must be executed with great control. This is a very powerful attack, so beware.

DEFENDER          ATTACKER

**1▲** Stand in ready stance, with the attacker in left-leg front stance, guard held in freestyle. Attacker: don't make your stance too wide or it will slow the spin.

**3◄** Now attack with front kick, to the attacker's mid-section. Remember to stay low and to drive both hips into the kick. Your earlier body-shift to 45 degrees has now opened up the attacker's centre line and you have a choice of target areas. The throat, stomach and groin are all now vulnerable.

**4▼** As the front kick snaps back, drive forward into front stance. As you land, attack with rising elbow strike, to the jaw.

**2◄** The attacker calls 'Ushiro Geri', then spins and attacks with back kick to the mid-section. Step back with your right leg and make downward block with the left arm. Don't step back in line with the kick, but step out at an angle of 45 degrees, so taking your body off line. This angle change is vital in creating a target area to strike at when you counter.

# Back kick (2)

In this final scenario we will see the
defender use a block not used previously:
a two-handed open-hand sweeping block.
It is particularly effective against kicks and
is a good way of knocking an attacker off
balance. Make sure you use the palms of
the hands to block. Let the kick come to
you, then deflect it. Don't slap at the leg.

**2▲** The attacker calls 'Ushiro
Geri', then spins and delivers
a right-leg back kick to the mid-
section. Step back with your left
leg and sweep the kick away
using the palms of both hands.
Use the attacker's spin to help
you take him round.

**3▶** As the attacker now lands,
right leg forward and hopefully
off balance, start to spin in
preparation for back kick with
the left leg. At this point, you
should already be looking at
the attacker and the target you
intend to hit. This is a midpoint
and should not be held for more
than a moment, or the attacker
will have time to evade.

DEFENDER    ATTACKER

**1▲** Stand in ready stance. The
attacker stands in left-leg front
stance, guard in freestyle position.

**4▶** Using the rotation of your body, now drive out a back kick into the attacker's mid-section. Make sure both hips go into the kick for full effect. The striking point is the heel and so is very powerful – control is vital.

---

**REMEMBER**
- **Never reach forwards to make the block – let the kick come to you and, at the last moment, deflect it.**
- **Time the block so that the palms of the hands connect with the ankle. If you don't get the timing right, and catch the calf area instead, the kick will probably hit you.**
- **This combination of counters is very difficult to put together. Start slowly and learn about distance and correct timing. When you have a grip on these skills, begin to add the power.**

**5▼** Once the kick has hit the target and is recovering, step forward into left-leg front stance and punch to the face with reverse punch.

# Training diary

# Index of techniques

*Please note:*
Full demonstrations of the techniques are shown in **bold**.

## Club contacts

If you're looking for a reputable club to train at, the internet is a useful source of information. Always look for JKA (Japan Karate Association) affiliated organizations – there are numerous sites for these, and most contain links listing club addresses, so you should be able to find one near to where you live.

## About the author

**Kevin Healy** has attained 5th Dan JKA. He began training in Shotokan Karate in 1977, and three years later was awarded black belt, 1st Dan. He continued training and passed his 5th Dan in May 1997. During this twenty-year period he was a member of both the KUGB junior and senior national squads. In 1989 he became EKB national kumite champion. Kevin trained with some of the true masters, Andy Sherry (7th Dan) and Keinosuke Enoeda (9th Dan), before becoming an instructor in his own right. He has been teaching for the last twenty years, and is a serving police officer with London's Metropolitan Police force.

EDDISON•SADD EDITIONS

**Editorial Director** Ian Jackson
**Senior Editor** Katie Golsby
**Art Director** Elaine Partington
**Designer** Malcolm Smythe
**Illustrator** Sheilagh Noble
**Production** Cara Herron